A Bit of a
ShemOzzle
GAA Quips and Quotes

MARTIN O'DUFFY

THE O'BRIEN PRESS
DUBLIN

First published 2017 by

The O'Brien Press Ltd,

12 Terenure Road East, Rathgar,

Dublin 6, D06 HD27 Ireland.

Tel: +353 1 4923333; Fax: +353 1 4922777

E-mail: books@obrien.ie

Website: www.obrien.ie

ISBN: 978-1-84717-953-1

1 3 5 7 8 6 4 2

17 19 21 20 18

Printed and bound in Poland by Białostockie Zakłady Graficzne S.A.

The quotations by Patrick Kavanagh are reprinted from 'Gut Yer Man' in *A Poet's Country:
Selected Prose*, edited by Antoinette Quinn (The Lilliput Press, 2003),
by kind permission of the Trustees of the Estate of the late Katherine B. Kavanagh,
through the Jonathan Williams Agency.

Thanks to Dara, and Joe, for their helpful advice and suggestions (and honest reactions) throughout the compiling and editing. Thanks to Donal, Tony and Oscar for casting their expert eyes over the text, and to Maedhbh and Damian for their advice on the title. And thanks to all at The O'Brien Press, particularly Helen and Emma, for getting the book over the line.

Special thanks to Micheál Ó Muircheartaigh, Liam Spratt, Jonathan Williams for The Patrick and Katherine Kavanagh Trust, and Conor Keane for the John B. Keane estate, for their time and generosity. And to all of those quoted in these pages, for their contribution to the uniquely entertaining world of GAA.

CONTENTS

Stand for the National Anthem

It is ordained and established that the commons of the said land of Ireland ... use not henceforth the games which men call 'hurlings' with great clubs at ball upon the ground, from which great evils and maims have arisen, to the weakening of the defence of the said land.

Statute of Kilkenny, 1366, bans English colonists from going native when it came to sport

At no time to use ne occupy ye hurling of ye litill balle with the hookie sticks or staves.

Galway, not to be out-done by the Cats, steps up with its Statute in 1527

When their cows are casting their hair, they pull it off their backs and with their hands work it into large balls which will grow very hard. This ball they use at the hurlings which they strike with a stick called the commaan…you may sometimes see one of the gamesters carry the ball tossing it for 40 or 50 yards in spite of all the adverse players.

John Dunton, English author, 1698

No person or persons whatsoever shall play, use or practise any hurling, communing, football playing … on the Lord's Day, or any part thereof; and if any person or persons shall offend therein [they] shall forfeit the sum of five pennies for every such offense.

Now we have *The Sunday Game*, then there was the Sunday Observance Act (1695)

Every effort has been made to make the meetings look as English as possible – foot races, betting and flagrant cheating being their most prominent features. Swarms of pot-hunting mashers sprang into existence.

Michael Cusack, co-founder of the GAA, calls for Irish management of national games

Dear Sir,
I received your letter this morning and burned it.
Yours faithfully,
Michael Cusack

The GAA co-founder's rebuke to the Irish Amateur Athletics Association's amalgamation proposal

And unfortunately it is not our national sports alone that are held in dishonour and dying out … Who hears now of snap-apple night or bonfire night? They are all things of the past, too vulgar to be spoken of except in ridicule by the degenerate dandies of the day.

Archbishop Thomas William Croke,
accepting patronage of the GAA

We cannot hurl very well when night sets in, but we can then cultivate our minds, and we know no better skill game better calculated to do this than the peaceable warlike game of chess … it was the principal instrument of culture among the most glorious people that ever lived in Ireland – the Fenians of ancient Erin.

Michael Cusack, who believed that the Irish not only invented hurling but also chess (with each of the thirty-two squares on the board representing an Irish county)

Young men assemble early on Sundays, sometimes to practise, sometimes to play ... many have no opportunity of hearing mass before leaving ...They draw after them the children of both sexes, thus depriving them of instruction in the Catechism. Yes and they draw after them too, foolish old men who would be better employed telling their beads in a quiet corner of the church and praying for the end which is so close upon them.

Archbishop Logue of Armagh, 1888
Down with this sort of thing.

Each of them took it in turn and kissed it with reverence, while all three wept copiously.

Pat Davin on the 1888 US tour by GAA sportsmen (the 'American Invasion'), and the reaction of three elderly Irish women to the hurley given to them by one of the players

Who has not heard that hurling is a dangerous game?
It is the most dangerous game ever played on the
planet … invented by the most sublimely energetic and
warlike race the world has ever known.

Michael Cusack
Hon the Cusack!

The men of Ireland were hurling when the gods of
Greece were young.

Attributed to PJ Devlin, early GAA activist

If the Sinn Féiners want their hurling to be free of
taxes, they can go into the trenches and hurl bombs.

**The unionist newspaper, the *Fermanagh Times*,
on a special tax break for the GAA
by the Asquith government in 1916**

Saturday May 15th: 'Not much sleep last night when Nealon and Kennedy called on their rounds with notebook and pencil, asked if we jazzed with the Germans, thereby suspending ourselves from the GAA, and if we took the meat sandwiches, thereby excommunicating ourselves from the Catholic Church'.

Journal entry from Thomas J Kenny's 1926 publication,
Tour of the Tipperary Hurling Team in America

The ground itself was like a car park, the field was 140 by 80 yards wide and because it was used for baseball there was the mound in the middle for the pitcher. We'd never seen anything like that before and we all thought this would have to be removed, but one of the Americans just gave us this stern look and said that it wasn't to be touched.

Teddy O'Sullivan, Kerry footballer, on GAA's Saipan moment during preparations for the 1947 All-Ireland final at New York's Polo Grounds

It wasn't something you'd trip over. You knew it was
there. I wouldn't think it put anyone out of their stride.
But when you came from a place like Kilnaleck in
Cavan you came across plenty of bad fields
and bad football pitches.
**Peter Donohoe, Cavan footballer and 1947 final
Man of the Match, on that 10-inch high and
18ft-diameter pitcher's mound**

And if there's anybody along the way there listening in,
just give us five minutes more!
**RTE's Michael O'Hehir, regarded by many as the original
GAA commentator, appeals to the New York operator to keep
the broadcast lines open as the 1947 final ran over. O'Hehir's
plea must have worked – a million radio listeners stayed
tuned to hear of Cavan's victory over Kerry
on American soil**

The GAA rule was simple: play rugby or football, and you were forbidden the joys of Gaelic football and hurling – and vice versa. We all *knew* it was ridiculous then, but in retrospect, it is almost impossible to believe. The rugby and football fields of Ireland were crawling with pseudonyms. Woe betide anyone who was found out! Expulsion and disgrace – and if the local parish priest could have you excommunicated from the Holy Roman Catholic Church, he would have, and *laughed* at your chances of salvation.

Terry Wogan, broadcaster, from his biography *Is It Me?*

I've always had a soft spot for the Irish, but ever since last Sunday I've been annoyed by them. Annoyed with them for keeping this great game of hurling to themselves for so long. Here is something as Irish as gaelic coffee. Yet you Irish have been shy and bashful about singing its praises to the rest of the world.

I wonder why?

Kenneth Wolstenholme, English sports commentator, 1959

Followers of football will be able to see a novel attraction at the Clonmel Sportsfield tonight (Thursday) at 8.30pm … The standard while it may not approach that of the Kerry mens [*sic*] team will prove an attraction in more ways than one.

Notice of a 'lovely girls' football match in 1969 between Clonmel Post Office and the County Council office staff

In many ways we were like the suffragettes of football trying to get recognition.

Marina Barry, former Kerry footballer, on the rise of women's gaelic football in the 70s and early 80s

Make way for that other All-Ireland …
Move over Heffo's Army,
the girls of Offaly and Tipperary are after
that All-Ireland Football crown.

Liam Kelly, *Evening Press*, on the first-ever Ladies All-Ireland final in 1974

Throw-In

The game is in and the ball is on.
Liam Spratt, South East Radio

In the first half they played with the wind, in the second half they played with the ball.
Micheál Ó Muircheartaigh, legendary RTE commentator

He may be bootless, he may be sockless, he may be stick-less, but he is certainly not ball-less.
Michael O'Hehir on Cork hurler Alan Lotty who, on a scorching hot day in Croker, discarded first his boots, then his socks, and later lost his hurl in a collision with another player

A nail came up through one boot. Now, you discard one boot and you're lopsided so you've to take off the second boot. And then the socks come down over your toes and begin to trip you up.
Babs Keating, Tipp hurler, on his barefoot performance in the 1971 All-Ireland final

Mike Sheehy was running up to take the kick – and suddenly Paddy [Cullen] dashed back towards his goal like a woman who smells a cake burning. The ball won the race and it curled inside the near post as Paddy crashed into the outside of the net and lay against it like a fireman who had returned to find his station ablaze.

Con Houlihan, sportswriter, on Kerry's Mikey Sheehy's lobbed goal while the Dublin goalie argued with the ref during the 1978 All-Ireland final

The greatest freak of all time.

Michael O'Hehir on the same goal

If I got a penny for every time that I was asked about it, I would be sunning it up over in the Bahamas now.

Mikey Sheehy himself has the last word

We may have come in the back door, but we're going
out the front.
**Hubert Rigney, Offaly hurling captain,
on their 1998 All-Ireland win**

As opticians, we understand that good vision is vital
to good sportsmanship and the integrity of referees'
decisions. Our sponsorship will ensure the
refs are seeing clearly.
**The ref *did* go to Specsavers! Seamus Breslin, Specsavers store
director, announces their 2010 sponsorship of the
Ladies Gaelic Football Association**

And the Jacks are back alright and the way they're
playing right now the Galway backs are jacked!
Michael O'Hehir on the 1974 football final

I looked at the scoreboard at one time and thought it
was the time: 4-17.
Darragh Ó Sé, former Kerry footballer

It's better as a player, but when you are forty-four
and two stone overweight and going slow,
winning as a manager isn't bad.
Páidí Ó Sé, former Kerry footballer and manager

In my day, we had a few farmers, a few fishermen and a
college boy to take the frees.
Paddy 'Bawn' Brosnan, Kerry footballer on 1940s tactics

I think that in life, if you keep hopping your head off a
stone wall, eventually you will get a break.
Nicky English, Tipperary hurling manager

Match of the decade, though that was no good to us
because we didn't win it.
**Eamonn Coleman, former Derry manager,
on his team's 1994 defeat to Down**

We had our Viagra at half-time.
**Niall Finnegan, after Galway turned around a flaccid
first-half performance to defeat Kildare and become the
1998 All-Ireland champions**

We'll have to send him a Christmas card or buy him a
pint somewhere along the line.
**Eamonn Fitzmaurice, Kerry football manager, in 2013
after Dublin's Paul Mannion equalised with Donegal,
keeping Kerry in Division 1**

Everyone is looking at women's Gaelic football as a
serious thing now. It's no joke anymore and it's not
a reason just to get the women out of the kitchen –
they're playing it because they want to win.
**Noreen Walsh, Waterford footballer, on the growing
significance of women's football in Ireland (1997)**

He kicks it from his hand with his left hand.
Ooooh, foot even.
Liam Spratt

Teddy looks at the ball, the ball looks at Teddy.
Micheál Ó Muircheartaigh

Don't always be looking at the end result, lads, enjoy
the road a little. That was one of the greatest spins you
could have there today. Good road,
breathtaking scenery, the lot.
**Ger Loughnane, Clare hurling manager, after his team's
thrilling 1999 quarter-final draw with Galway**

To win in September you have to suffer in January.
Brian Corcoran, Cork dual player

Janey, lads, will ya get the ball out, ye divils, ye? Will
ye kick the ball out?! ... Jesus, what are you doing?
Will you drive the ball down the field, or what are you
doing? ... Ger, what are you doing, Ger? You're holding
on to it! Jaysus, will you give it off? ... Jesus, 'tis terrible.
C'mon, lads, kick that ball! ... Ah for Jaysus' sake, that's
a f**kin' penalty! Ya bollocks! Jay ...
I'm going to collapse!
Effin' Eddie Moroney commenting on the
1992 Tipperary U21 B final between Aherlow and Nenagh

I kind of mis-hit it and that maybe put the keeper off.
But sure it counts the same as a screamer!
Jonjo Farrell, Kilkenny hurler, proves a goal is a goal

Teddy McCarthy to John McCarthy (no relation). John McCarthy back to Teddy McCarthy (still no relation).
Micheál Ó Muircheartaigh

If we gathered up twenty at the Red Cow and came down this morning, it could hardly have been worse.
Anthony Daly, Dublin hurling manager, blasts his team's poor performance in the 2012 Leinster semi-final

Like trying to climb Mount Everest when you've been practising on Carrauntuohil.
Donal O'Grady, Limerick hurling manager, on the change in gear from Division 2 to the Munster Championship semi-final

He hits it. He hits it! It's over the baaaaaar!
Oh Holy Moses, what a match!
I have never experienced anything like it.
RTE's Marty Morrissey on the 2013 hurling final

1-5 to 0-8. Well, from Lapland to the Antarctic, that's
level scores in any man's language.
Micheál Ó Muircheartaigh

May the best horse jump the ditch and
we'll see what happens.
Davy Fitzgerald, Clare hurling manager

You should be so close to the Corner Forward
that when he goes to scratch his arse
'tis your arse he's scratching.
Christy 'Cra' Murray, Sixmilebridge

Well, the game is on with one team. Barney Rock in possession, fourteen yards out and he's scored a goal. No goalkeeper. The green flag is waved by the umpire. The referee did throw in the ball. Dublin leading by one goal but they're playing against nobody here in Croke Park at the moment.

Micheál Ó Muircheartaigh commenting on Dublin's win over Cork in the 1987 football league quarter-final. At the final whistle the teams were level, and Cork management refused to let their team take to the pitch for extra time.

There's no Cork team here. There it is. Dublin the only team on the field. This is absolutely ridiculous. Barney Rock with no opposition. The first, the only time I have seen this at Croke Park. Dublin score a goal and presumably this absolutely farcical end to a football game proves conclusively that Dublin are the team to qualify – at least in the referee's opinion and the fans' view – for the semi-finals.

Ger Canning's view on the same match, recorded for RTE's *Sports Special*

Thank you very much indeed, gentlemen, for keeping us right up to date with that story. It's a great one for the quiz, isn't it? How many players had Cork on the field when Barney Rock scored the winning goal in 1987?

Answer: zero!

RTE's Jimmy Magee has the final word

We seemed to be like startled earwigs in the first fifteen minutes.

Pat Gilroy, Dublin football manager, on their 2009 defeat to Kerry

Dublin have scored two points, one from the hand and one from the land.

Micheál Ó Muircheartaigh, part-time poet

Hurling is the Riverdance of sport.

Liam Griffin, Wexford hurling manager

There was a lot of loose marking and stuff like that in the years before. When Páidí [Ó Sé] was finished he made sure that lads were nearly down another man's pants.

Denis Glennon, Westmeath footballer

Colm O'Rourke: Maybe they're trying to keep Laois
waiting in the sun, a bit like Kerry last year.
Joe Brolly: Or maybe they're sitting in there
with some custard creams.

**RTE's *The Sunday Game* pundits on Armagh's delayed return
after half-time of the 2003 football quarter-final**

We don't have shares in it, anyway,
if that's what you're asking.

**Brian Cody, Kilkenny hurling manager, when asked about
Hawkeye's call against a point for Waterford**

A goal! A great goal for Wexford. Fantastic goal there,
Ned. I didn't see the goal or who scored it as I was
talking to Liam Griffin. Did you see the goal, Ned?

Liam Spratt

He grabs the slíotar. He's on the 50. He's on the 40.
He's on the 30! He's on the ground!
Micheál Ó Muircheartaigh

Never take your eyes off the ball –
even when it's in the referee's pocket.
Christy Ring, Cork hurler

You look at Sheedy on the sideline and
he's doing Riverdances.
**Babs Keating, former Tipp hurling manager
on his successor Liam Sheedy**

I hold my hands up to say McGeeney and O'Rourke and company totally out-tacticalled us on the night.

Justy McNulty, Laois football manager and linguist, on his team's defeat by Kildare

Every man, woman and monkey didn't give them a chance.

David Brady, former Mayo footballer and GAA blogger, on Mayo's 2011 victory over Cork

He kicks the ball ard san aer. Could've been a goal, could've been a point ... it went wide.

Micheál Ó Muircheartaigh

A championship game is like a bungee jump that lasts for seventy minutes. The enjoyment only comes when you're unstrapped and you look back up and say 'I did that. How the f**k did I do it?'
Declan Darcy, Leitrim & Dublin footballer

The goals killed us.
All 8 of them. **Barney Breen, Leitrim football manager, after their defeat to Armagh 8-13 to 10 points**

All Stars

He's one of those players you'll stand naked
in the snow to watch.
Martin Carney, RTE, on Monaghan footballer Paul Finlay

Seán Óg Ó'Hailpín – his father's from Fermanagh, his
mother from Fiji, neither a hurling stronghold.
Micheál Ó Muircheartaigh

He was complicated. You never knew what to expect.
He was a divil, like.
Marty Morrissey on Páidí Ó Sé

We were eating Weetabix, but your man was eating
dumbbells for breakfast.
**Tomás Mulcahy, former Cork hurler,
on Larry Tompkins, Cork football captain**

He's not the loveable type of manager. But none are.
Conor Mortimer, former Mayo footballer,
on manager James Horan

My mother is acting as a stand-in agent.
Shane O'Donnell, Clare hurler, on the newfound attention
he received after his hat-trick during his team's
2013 All-Ireland win

I just hope Shane O'Donnell is single. The man has the
busiest winter of his life ahead of him. He can delete
his Tinder account.
Michael Conroy, Mayo footballer, tweets about O'Donnell's
dating prospects after that hat-trick

Eoin Liston, their lofty target man, the pine tree in
whose branches they hoped the long high ball
would stick.
Con Houlihan on the Kerry footballer

Donaghys don't grow on trees.
Liam Kearns, Laois football manager,
on Kerry's Kieran Donaghy

... [the] local paper [said] ... we were all Trojans in
defence and wizards in attack. I once got a lot of kudos
from a report which described me as 'incisive around
goal'. No one knew the meaning of the word incisive
but it sounded good.
Patrick Kavanagh, poet

With young lads coming on the block, we older fellas decided we'd give them good example. So we actually gave up the drink that year. We gave it up on the Tuesday night before the match.

Noel Lane, former Galway hurler, on preparations for the 1985 semi-final against Cork

That's not the face of an international football star, that's a minor hurler from Offaly who got lucky.

Dara Ó Briain, comedian and presenter, on soccer star Wayne Rooney

Danny 'The Yank' Culloty – he has come from San Francisco and hasn't he done well?

Micheál Ó Muircheartaigh on the US-born Cork midfielder

He has a left foot in the right place.
Colm O'Rourke, former Meath footballer and RTE analyst,
on Down's Benny Coulter

He's not a big man, he's not a small man.
He's what you might call a handy man.
Micheál Ó Muircheartaigh

I get slagging that I'm not as good as the mother.
Cork hurler Seamus Harnedy gets a hard time from his
UCC teammates over his mother Cathy's (née Landers) six
All-Ireland camogie medals

Gerry cleared the first few balls and Ring came down and tapped him on the back, 'Young Browne, I have heard of you.' Now, Gerry said he grew two feet there and then, but when he looked again, Ring was over in the far corner, took possession and stuck it in the net. Ring came back over, tapped him again and said 'You need to keep a much closer eye on me.'

Tom McNamara, Crusheen club stalwart,
on Clare hurler Gerry Browne meeting the legend,
Christy Ring

To some of these fans, Christy Ring is a roundabout on the outer ring road.

Tony Connelly, former Cork hurler

If a man who fishes for salmon with a stage net had
seen his cordage dance as often as Paddy Cullen did …
he would have been very happy indeed
with his day's work.

Con Houlihan on the Dublin goalkeeper

I asked the mother to lock him in the bedroom on
Sunday morning, but she wouldn't do it. I might have
to go up there and do it myself the next time.

**Kilkenny hurling legend Tommy Walsh on losing his county's
number five jersey to his little brother Padraig**

And Tom Cheasty breaks through with Kilkenny
defenders falling around him like dying wasps.
Michael O'Hehir on the Waterford hurling centre-forward

I don't know where my mind was at. That backwards
handpass was a bit flamboyant.
**Clare hurler Pádraic 'Podge' Collins plays down
a show of skill against Galway**

Colin Corkery on the 45 lets go with the right boot.
It's over the bar! This man shouldn't be playing football!
He's made an almost Lazarus-like recovery from a heart
condition! Lazarus was a great man but he couldn't kick
points like Colin Corkery.
Micheál Ó Muircheartaigh on the Cork footballer

They're one behind. Will he put it over the bar to draw it, or go for the win? It happened here in an O'Donoghue Cup final many years ago. Paud O'Donovan from Glenflesk had a penalty and he stood up and put it in the net. I was reporting for Radio Kerry and I asked him afterwards did he think about putting it over the bar. He said, 'Weeshie, the replay would be on next weekend and I'm going on my holidays so I wasn't taking the chance'.

Weeshie Fogarty, Radio Kerry

He's a better player than Cooper, in my opinion.
He's one of the greatest I've ever seen. In my opinion,
Cooper is a two-trick pony but that lad there is
a six- or seven-trick pony.

**Martin McHugh, former Donegal footballer and
Cavan manager, compares Kerry's James O'Donoghue
to fellow county man Colm 'the Gooch' Cooper.**

OMG!! I keep saying she's a legend!

**RTE's Des Cahill sings the praises of Mayo footballer
Cora Staunton after she scored 5-15 for club Carnacon
in the 2016 county final**

The Michael Jordan of hurling.

ESPN commentator on Cork hurler Donal Óg Cusack

To be honest, I don't like watching fellows doing things
which I sometimes feel I could still do better myself.
**Former Cork hurler Larry Flaherty on watching games
in the 1970s (while he was in his 90s).
Flaherty learned to hurl using a sycamore branch and a can.**

ANYBODY who takes more than their share of
sausages/goujons after matches will run laps.
ANYBODY who posts on social media and
does not finish their post with #hontheyard
will be banned from the club for life.
ATTENDANCE of Electric Picnic this year
has been banned. Nathan Carter's concerts
have been approved with the manager's consent.
**Laois club Crettyard's parody contract pokes fun
at the increasing demands on players**

Cork's elite sportsmen walk a perilous line between unshakeable confidence and unfailing modesty. Their public's ideal hero is a player of Godlike grace; a swaggering apparition of athletic transcendence capable of lowering the heavens or at least raising the Earth. And off the field he will have the humility of an 80-year-old lollipop lady.
Jimmy Barry-Murphy in other words.
Ronan Early, *Irish Post*

[Brian Cody's] record is really unbelievable. I've already pigeoned him to have a chat with him later on to see if we can try and get a result against Scotland between us.
Martin O'Neill, Republic of Ireland soccer manager

We often say in Galway:
if only we had two more Thereses.
Sharon Glynn, Galway camogie player,
on team mate Therese Maher

[Shane Curran] comes from that great dramatic tradition of out-of-your-box crazy goalkeepers, and he could save a penalty and score a 45, but at the same time he'd be just as happy to ride a bull into a church, and he could do all of those things in the space of two hours. He was gangbusters ... I would have been the minor keeper while he was the senior keeper ...
He was a law unto himself.
Chris O'Dowd, actor, writer, and late 1990s Roscommon minor football goalie

Neither of us are that brave that we'd wear the bib in his absence!
Michael Dempsey, Kilkenny hurling selector, on himself and Martin Fogarty stepping in for manager Brian Cody during the 2013 league

Anthony Lynch, the Cork corner back, will be the last person to let you down; his people are undertakers.

Micheál Ó Muircheartaigh

He can take the ball from one end of the field to the other with just the player's occupations.

Kerry footballer Jack O'Shea on Micheál Ó Muircheartaigh

Gooch that day of the All-Ireland final. That time is burned into my head. 1:50pm, less than two hours to the biggest day of our lives and he's fast asleep in the hotel bed. When I woke him, he had a stretch. He has that coolness. It's cold.

**Kerry footballer Paul Galvin
on teammate Colm 'the Gooch' Cooper**

I remember once hearing about how he had jumped
so high to make a catch, that his boots tripped over his
opponent's shoulders.

Gerry McGovern, *Hot Press,*
on Kerry football legend Mick O'Connell

I was waiting under a dropping ball with Phil Stuart of
Derry when I caught a glimpse of a pair of knees above
my shoulder and hands gripping the ball.

It was Mick O'Connell.

Seamus Murphy, former Kerry footballer

I was taught geography for four years by
Colm O'Rourke … this was back when Colm was
winning All-Irelands for Meath … Colm would
come into school on Monday, covered in medals and
bandages, like Navan's answer to Tarzan …
this Cúchulainn of a man.

Tommy Tiernan, comedian, on RTE's *Late, Late Show*

None. But I was out threshing until 10 o'clock every
night. What training would I need?
Paddy Martin, Kildare footballer in the 1920s & 30s

Yeah, I was working this morning. It's what I do every
day and I like to stick to normality so I milked the
cows this morning [all 400 of them].
**Briege Corkery, Cork dual player on her preparation
for the 2016 football semi-final**

I always had great self-conviction and I think it is really
important to have confidence in yourself
and don't give a damn.
Jack O'Shea, Kerry footballer

It used to be a good old Ulster fry before matches, but we've changed that now to muesli – which tastes a wee bit like what you'd find at the bottom of a budgie's cage.

Benny Tierney, Armagh goalkeeper, unimpressed with manager Big Joe's health-kick

Setanta Ó hAilpín ... the original Setanta from the old Gaelic stories was ten foot tall, but even he couldn't be playing better hurling than his namesake here today.

Micheál Ó Muircheartaigh on the Cork hurler

It was a bit strange. You'd have to go into a separate dressing room. None of the boys wanted to mark me. They definitely didn't want to mark me after I scored a couple of goals.

Cora Staunton on her early days playing on mixed teams

Pat Fox has it on his hurl and is motoring well now.
But here comes Joe Rabbitte hot on his tail.
I've seen it all now! A rabbit chasing a fox.
**Micheál Ó Muircheartaigh on the Tipp fox
and the Galway rabbit**

You'd want a great pair of legs to keep up a big head –
and he hasn't those either.
**Jack Lynch, Taoiseach and holder of six consecutive
All-Ireland medals (five in hurling, one in football), does not
hold back in his description of a player**

On match days you'd go into the dressing room, the
lads'd be banging the hurl off the table, they'd be
psyching. I'd go in, tap the ball off the shower wall, get
togged out and then go in and just have the last fag.
**Johnny Pilkington, former Offaly hurler,
on that vital pre-match prep**

I set in place a personal training programme. Fairly primitive stuff, mind you … Regularly, I would set off over the Clasach, run down into Dún Chaoin, and around by Slea Head back to Ventry. Fourteen miles of the hardest, ball-breaking terrain you can run.

Páidí Ó Sé

I never retired. They just stopped picking me.

Tony Scullion, Derry footballer

I've always loved John Newton because I've always thought that the greatest skill in Gaelic football is fielding the ball and he did it with such gusto, such kind of majesty, he'd jump up like a randy salmon from the field and pluck a star.

Chris O'Dowd on the Roscommon footballer

County

Colours

Beating Kerry in the All-Ireland was always
a double All-Ireland to me.
Kevin Heffernan, Dublin football manager

We had to work very hard for this. It took 119 years for
us to get it.
Mickey Harte, Tyrone football manager, after his team's
2003 All-Ireland win

I don't think Kilkenny have a player who is unhurlable.
Daithí Regan, former Offaly hurler

And the ball is hit in … and and it's a goal for Wexford!
And when I say Wexford of course I mean Laois.

Liam Spratt

In all the years that I had been hurling for Wexford the man above wasn't on our side. He wasn't even giving us a fair chance, he didn't even give us a fifty-fifty.

Martin Storey, Wexford hurler,
on making it to the 1996 All-Ireland final

Sure you know the Mayo hurlers haven't been beaten west of the Shannon in the last twenty years.

A somewhat dubious claim made in the movie
The Quiet Man **(1952)**

Down's plan last year was to kick the ball to Benny Coulter, and if that didn't work to kick it even more to Benny Coulter.

Colm O'Rourke

Kilkenny hurlers? We'll see your four and raise you one.
All-Ireland-winning Cork football captain
Mary O'Connor in her five-in-a-row acceptance speech, 2009

With them bastards of mountains in front of us, and
those hoors of lakes behind us, sure there's nothing to
do but play football.
Jackie Lyne, Kerry footballer

They're not eating any more spuds or anything than
anybody else and if you start to believe that they're
invincible, then sure look, don't get involved in sport.
Sean Boylan, ex-Meath football manager, on the growing
dominance of Dublin

Donegal might have been waiting for a hundred years to come here. The Four Masters history might have ended in 1616 but Donegal of '92 are there with Dublin's Jack Sheedy attacking. He's got the ball, 30 yards out. A long kick from Jack Sheedy that looks a beauty. It's gone over the bar by Jack Sheedy, 35 yards out on the right wing and that's two for Jack Sheedy. I was telling you about the Four Masters in 1616. They completed a history of Ireland ... wish they were here, Donegal people would say, to chronicle this.

Micheál Ó Muircheartaigh on Donegal's first appearance in an All-Ireland final, top-notch commentary with a little extra

There's a lot of satisfaction because there were times we were really written off. Fellas like Spillane there now, were almost taking pity on us. He was thinking there wasn't even one dying kick in us!

**Jack O'Connor, Kerry football manager,
on their 2009 All-Ireland win**

Dublin would have fully deserved a draw
if they had won.

Liam Spratt

In certain minds, it's always chains and ashes. Especially
in places like Wexford and Clare. 'Jaysus, boy, we
dragged tractors through bogs.' It's a load of nonsense.
You wouldn't win an All-Ireland doing that.

**Liam Griffin on the importance of training being
90 per cent hurling**

I'm not giving away any secrets like that to Tipperary.
If I had my way, I wouldn't even tell them
the time of the throw-in.

Ger Loughnane

1948 is a long time ago. Sean T O'Kelly was the president, John A Costello was the Taoiseach, he took over from Éamon de Valera, Noel Browne was the Minister for Health and it's all over! Waterford are All-Ireland champions for a third time, the first time since 1948. Waterford hurling is back on the big stage!

Kieran O'Connor, WLR FM, effortlessly combines Irish history with sporting history

Being beaten.

Nigel Higgins, former Wexford hurler, on his memories of games against Kilkenny

The hurling final was as near a perfect display of hurling as you can get and though Clare gave Kilkenny a determined and brave run I had sympathy with the despondent Clare fan who said 'You know, it would take two teams to beat Kilkenny'.

President Mary McAleese on the 2002 All-Ireland final

Des Cahill: Did you have to explain to the English what hurling was about?

Dara Ó Briain: No, but I have to explain it to the people of Wicklow.

RTE's Des Cahill with Dara Ó Briain, comedian, presenter and staunch hurling fan, whose own playing career peaked with a half-hour stint in a league match for the Wicklow minors

Walking along Banna Beach on a Friday and heading off with Kerry on a Saturday afternoon to Croke Park – it's like going to battle and I feel that I've got to protect what I've left behind in Kerry.

Paul Galvin

Dublin tactics: hit high ball into box and wait for Mayo 'curse' to do the rest.

A tweet from columnist Billy Tyson

Meath are like Dracula: they're never dead 'til there's a
stake through their heart.

Martin Carney

If Wexford Hurling Ltd was a company and we had
produced the results that we have over the last
twenty-five years or so, we would have been declared
bankrupt long ago.

Phil Murphy, *Wexford People*

Kilkenny don't do tactics, the Pope isn't Catholic and
bears use bidets.

Donal Óg Cusack, former Cork hurler

I'm not a huge hurling fan but I suppose, like any
Wexford person, I was a hurling fan that year.
Eoin Colfer, author, on Wexford's 1996 All-Ireland glory

The team who beat the team who couldn't be beaten.
Pete McGrath, Down football manager,
at the team's homecoming after beating Meath
in the 1991 All-Ireland final

Dublin in rare new times.
Irish Times **headline after a shock win by**
Dublin hurlers in 2007

A Kerry footballer with an inferiority complex is one
who thinks he's just as good as everybody else.
John B. Keane, playwright and novelist

This is the only Mayoman who honeymooned
in the Himalayas!
Micheál Ó Muircheartaigh peppering his commentary
with a little inside information

When Ger Loughnane was over Galway, a 10-point loss
to Kilkenny was probably the highlight.
Ollie Canning, Galway hurler, pulls no punches

I'd wear a pink g-string if Mayo were to
win the All-Ireland.
David Brady

If Offaly ever win the National League again, it will be
the greatest accident since the *Titanic*.
Paul O'Kelly, former Offaly football manager

Hell hath no fury like an Ulster football supporter.
Joe Brolly, former Derry footballer and RTE analyst

We said this year the only team that's going to beat us
is ourselves, the A's and B's. And the second best team
in the country this year was our B team.
Philly McMahon, Dublin footballer,
following their 2015 All-Ireland win

There are really only two football teams in Ireland:
Dublin and Anywhere But Dublin.
David Slattery, Kildare footballer

If Dublin win, it's over-hyped.
If Dublin lose, it's over-hyped.
Ciarán Whelan, Dublin footballer

You could write the Meath tactics on the back of a postage stamp – just kick it up there. Some people would say it's bogman football.

Colm O'Rourke

Kerry against Dublin… The game where Corkonians wrestle with their consciences, trying to figure out who they most want to lose.

Donal O'Driscoll, *Cork Independent*

When Tyrone and Armagh people boast of the four senior All-Irelands they have won between them… you point out that three brothers from Ard an Bhóthair have 15 between them.

**A reminder from TheScore Team on The42.ie
about Kerry brothers
Darragh, Tomás and Marc Ó Sé**

Satellite news channel coverage of

Euro 2004 in Lisbon:

Reporter: Are you disappointed that England lost?

Waterford man: Not at all, I'm Irish, I'm from Waterford.

Reporter: But would you not support England when Ireland are not in the competition?

Waterford man: Jaysus, no way.

Reporter: Why not?

Waterford man: 800 years of oppression!

Reporter: Is there ever any time you would support England?

Waterford man: Maybe if they were playing Kilkenny!

A Grá for
the Game

I always had a grá for it. Many a cow was milked to a tight game in the cowshed!

Willie Hegarty, Shannonside Radio

Some people say hurling isn't very important in the scheme of things. But to hurling people, hurling *is* the scheme of things.

Ger Loughnane

There are some things in life that are more important than money and the GAA is one of them.

Joe Brolly

Somebody has said that no man can adequately describe Irish life who ignores the Gaelic Athletic Association, which is true in a way, for football runs women a hard race as a topic of conversation.

Patrick Kavanagh

When my friends were besotted with Jason Donovan,
my heroes were Colm O'Rourke and Barney Rock.
Sue Ramsbottom, Laois football captain

In Kerry I would have no hesitation in saying that
people's priorities go like this – family first,
Kerry football second and maybe religion third.
Weeshie Fogarty

I saw a few Sligo people at mass in Gardiner Street this
morning and omens seem to be good for them: the
priest was wearing the same colours as the Sligo jersey!
40 yards out on the Hogan-stand side of the field,
Ciaran Whelan goes on a run, it's a goal!
So much for omens.
Micheál Ó Muircheartaigh

Thank God we went to Knock on Saturday on the way.
Paul Coggins, London football manager, counts his blessings after their 2013 win over Leitrim

People have been asking me to pray for Sixmilebridge in today's county final, but I'm not going to because if we can't beat Newmarket decent there is no point in beating them at all.
Fr Harry Bohan, parish priest and former hurling manager

The All-Ireland final will beat any World Cup final or European final, trust me. Not that I've been to a World Cup final, but I've been to a few Champions' League finals.
Roy Keane, former Republic of Ireland soccer international

It's impossible to give 110 per cent unless you are to give up your job and leave your wife.

David Brady

Schoolwork was grand, but hurling was sacred.

Eoin Colfer, from his children's novel, *Benny and Omar*

Every morning we would go down to Croker …
We had no season tickets but hard necks, and the groundsmen knew us well. Knew us well enough to know that if we weren't let in we'd get in by devious routes and holes only wide enough to accommodate very young sportsmen, three or four feet tall, and about half a hundred-weight.

Brendan Behan, author, from
'My earliest memory of Croke Park',
Cuchulainn Annual

The death notices and the GAA are the two most
important things on local radio
Willie Hegarty

I keep some sheep myself, so when I want to relax I
head away up the hill away from everything. I'm into
the two businesses that don't pay: sheep and football.
Michael Hegarty, Donegal footballer

It's important to remember this is only part of the
person's life. He's a sportsman first of all –
they're All Stars, not porn stars!
**Senator David Norris reminds us that
GAA should be about the ball, not the balls.**

I love football, I don't just like it. You can't just like it.
John Maughan, Mayo football manager

There is nothing even vaguely intellectual about a
Munster hurling final, yet a proper enjoyment of the
game presupposes a sophisticated appreciation
of the finer things.
David Hanly, journalist and broadcaster, writing in
Ireland of the Welcomes

A fan is a person who, when you have made an idiot of
yourself on the pitch, doesn't think you've done
a permanent job.
Jack Lynch

I love Cork so much that if I caught one of their
hurlers in bed with my missus I'd tiptoe downstairs and
make him a cup of tea.
Joe Lynch, actor

Our boys being so good looking, and of course such heroes in the eyes of the fair sex, attract quite a number of fair ladies to the vicinity of their training quarters every evening and as a result we have some 'tripping in the light fantastic toe' which is all very well in its own way, taken in moderation ... but it should not come off every night and on no account be prolonged after ten.

From a letter to the *Clare Champion* on the county's preparations for the 1914 hurling final

It was GAA porn yesterday without a doubt.

David Brady

The most important nine months of a woman's life ... January to September.

Accompanying a photo of a Ladies Gaelic player in full kit, cradling a ball at her stomach – an ad campaign that TG4 wisely decided against using for their coverage of Ladies Gaelic Football

If you won the lottery, it wouldn't give you as much pleasure as Kildare have given both myself and other people for the last number of years; it's better than winning the lottery … it's better than sex.

Charlie McCreevy, then Minister for Finance

The difference between winning a club and a county All-Ireland is when you get a slap on the back after the match, you actually know the person when you turn around.

Tomás Meehan, former Galway and Caltra footballer

He's a peculiar fish at the best of times. He just needs a bit of love every now and again.

Bernard Brogan, Dublin footballer, on captain Stephen Cluxton

Babs Keating said to me one night, the difference between a pat on the back and a kick in the arse is a foot and a half.

Brian Kerr,
Republic of Ireland soccer manager

My nana collapsed and my Dad rang for an ambulance … and who arrives in the ambulance only Charlie Redmond [working as a paramedic] … Charlie brings her out to the ambulance and says 'Is there anybody you need to call?' And my Dad says 'I'll call my brother.' Then my Ma overheard him [on the phone], 'Yeah, look, it's Mick. You'll never believe who's in the house. It's Charlie Redmond, and you're gonna have to hurry over!'

Al Porter, comedian, talking on RTE's *Late, Late Show*
about his family's brush with Dublin footballing royalty

At last year's All-Ireland football final, I was overjoyed that Dublin showed such confidence: that's what the city lacked when I was a child. Leaving Croke Park with my expensive ticket stub, I remembered the old days, when Dad would hurl me over the turnstile to get me in as a junior, something he did until I was eighteen … An old Mayo man who recognised me asked was I a Mayo supporter. I told him I wasn't, and he said matter-of-factly, 'F**k you then, Sean. F**k you.' He made it sound welcoming, and I felt proud.

**Sean Hughes, comedian and writer,
on the 2013 Dublin v Mayo All-Ireland final**

Love of football can bring a special madness to the fore
in normally sane citizens

Brendan Kennelly, poet and novelist, in a eulogy
for renowned football fan John B. Keane
in the *Irish Independent*

I got pneumonia watching (for what you could see
of them) Kilkenny and Limerick, in the hurling final
of 1935, because there was a priest sitting beside me,
and he asked, when I got up to leave, whether I was
made of sugar. I thought he had given me dispensation
against rain…anyway, he'd lifted me over the sideline
from below Hill 16 and I didn't like to desert him.

Brendan Behan, author, from
'My earliest memory of Croke Park',
Cuchulainn Annual

A Shemozzle
in the
Parallelogram

Sometimes if he misses his blow at the ball, he knocks one of the opposers down, at which no resentment is to be shown. They seldom come off without broken heads or shins in which they glory very much.

John Dunton on the hurling he saw played in 1698

We never finished a game if towards the end we were 'a-batin. We always found an excuse to rise a row and get the field invaded.

Patrick Kavanagh

We were walking down the corridor with Mr Haughey who was on crutches at the time. He said to him 'Páidí, did you break any bones during your career?' and he said, 'Yes, Taoiseach, but none of my own.'

Sean Walsh, former Kerry GAA chairman, on Páidí Ó Sé

We're becoming too pansyish about our football.
It's a game for men, for God's sake.
Mick O'Dwyer, former Kerry player and manager,
on the increased number of sendings-off

He [John Hoyne] was warming up in the dressing
room and ... he got a slap of a hurl in the head from
someone. He got four staples before he went out ...
That was just the warm-up.
Henry Shefflin, Kilkenny hurler,
after his team won the 2002 All-Ireland final

The worst thing about the game was there wasn't even a
chance of a row.
Colm O'Rourke

Doctor: You will be in a sling for three or four weeks and absolutely no physical contact for six months.

Larry Tompkins: Six months??! The replay is in two weeks!

The Cork and Castlehaven footballer after the 1994 county final against O'Donovan Rossa, during which Tompkins snapped his collarbone. He went on to play with the victorious Castlehaven in the replay.

Coming towards the end of the summer … there'd be Gaelic matches on one channel and soccer on the other and you see fella's getting slapped with a hurl across the face and they just say 'G'wan – do it again, do it again' and then you see the wind change direction in a soccer match and eight of them fall down.

Tommy Tiernan on RTE's *The Tommy Tiernan Show*

An honest sport where men give and take the hard knocks and get on with it.
Shay Given, Republic of Ireland soccer international, on Gaelic football

[By the time they] have cleared up [doctors'] fees for the battle with Clonaslee we may go bankrupt.
Bob O'Keeffe, Laois hurler, after a particularly heated 1914 club match between Kilcotton and Clonaslee

Journalist: How's the leg, Kevin?
Kevin Moran: It's f**k ... it's very sore.
Kevin Moran, Dublin footballer and later Ireland soccer international, after the 1978 All-Ireland final against Kerry

It is, only you wouldn't see Kasparov taking Karpov and dragging him across the table and down the turf as he was about to checkmate him.

Joe Brolly, when fellow pundit Pat Spillane suggested a match was like a chess game

The intensity of the Ulster Championship sometimes makes the Colosseum look like a bouncy castle.

Tony Davis, former Cork footballer

It was like going to war. You just didn't care what was going to happen to yourself individually. It was the only time I ever understood how soldiers could go into battle and not be afraid of dying.

The cup meant nothing. This was personal …
it was war without bullets.

Ger Loughnane on the 1998 Munster hurling final

The more stitches required after a game in the Cork
dressing room, the more probable they had won.
Dr Con Murphy, Cork hurling team doctor

It's kind of handbag stuff, really.
**Tomás Mulcahy, former Cork hurler,
on a shemozzle in the tunnel before the
2007 Munster quarter final**

If there is an injury, don't try to describe it…
particularly a head injury. The player's mother or wife
or family might be listening and an ill-informed or
exaggerated comment could cause them unnecessary
worry. Always remember the listener. Now, off you go.
**Michael O'Hehir's advice to the young
Micheál Ó Muircheartaigh before his first
full commentary in 1962**

You get more contact in an old time waltz at an old folk's home than in a National League final.

Pat Spillane, former Kerry footballer and RTE analyst

But there's defenders being dragged down coming out with the ball by skilful corner-forwards who couldn't tackle a fish supper and are getting away with six or seven of them a game and nobody wants to issue them a black card!

**Kieran McGeeney, Kildare manager
and former Armagh footballer**

I didn't realise it was as bad, and then I saw it and I realised that, yeah, it's like a scene from *Gladiator*.

**Liam Rushe, Dublin hurler, on pulling across
Cork's Pa Horgan in the 2013 All-Ireland semi-final**

Crusheen used to come out of hurling matches with more injuries than you'd witness in the Battle of the Somme.

Tom McNamara

They were all queuing up to go 'I am Spartacus!'

Joe Brolly, on the controversy surrounding
Sean Cavanagh's foul on Conor McManus
in the 2013 Tyrone v Monaghan quarter-final

I always wore a helmet, gum shield and shin guards, but I learned the hard way. Nobody wants to lose too many teeth.

Angela Downey, former Kilkenny camogie player,
in an interview with writer Turtle Bunbury

It was like being hit by a bus or a train …
whichever is worse.

**James Horan, Mayo football manager, in 2013 after losing
their second All-Ireland final in a row**

Broke a few bones along the way alright. Broke a few
fingers. Broke my nose a couple of times lately. I tore
my cruciate in 2003 but didn't have the operation until
2008. I had my jaw broken in a colleges' game.
That was it, really.

Cora Staunton

The only time I heard tell of a hamstring was one
hanging in the window of St. John's butchers.

Mickey 'the Rattler' Byrne, former Tipp hurler

It wasn't a hard decision not to appeal…I was wrong to do what I did so I felt it best to take it on the chin.

Paul Galvin on his suspension for attempting to feed Cork's Eoin Cadogan a finger in the 2010 Munster football semi-final

The ball was introduced and dutifully ignored, as was the case with most Meath-Dublin clashes.

Dessie Farrell, Dublin footballer

I remember our good friend, Tom Mac being a selector at one time. He came in with a manure bag over his shoulder that was full of hurleys. He threw the bag down in the middle of the floor and he said 'Lads, I want to be able to roll this up and put it in my pocket on the way home.' In other words, don't spare them.

Jackie O'Gorman, former Clare hurler, on Tom McNamara

The umpire came out at this stage but, in his wisdom, he removed himself again. At this case, I mean, it's everyone is at it … In the background you can see some wonderful punches as well. A couple of great examples of slow waltzes … a nice little sumo wrestling impersonation here …

Pat Spillane on the brawl during the 1996 Meath v Mayo final replay, which Meath went on to win (the match, not the brawl)

I had to do a bit of ducking and diving … I ducked once and dived twice.

David Brady, former Mayo footballer, on his memory of the same match

And it looks like there's a bit of a shemozzle in the parallelogram.

Michael O'Hehir

Let every blow be a funeral. I don't want to see you coming back in here with dirty jerseys; I want to see you coming back in here with blood-stained jerseys. I know what they're thinking ... Oh, they're saying 'Timmy Ryan, Timmy Ryan. Timmy Ryan is too hard on us.' Well, I'll tell you something, lads, I'm not. And you'll know all about it next year when you're playing Under 14, right?

Jon Kenny as D'Unbelievables' Timmy Ryan, fictitious club manager, on the trials and tribulations of juvenile football

He'll regret this to his dying day, if he lives that long.

Dublin fan after Charlie Redmond's missed penalty in the 1994 All-Ireland final

Ye know it's GAA season again when there's lads going around the nightclub on crutches.

Lauren McGinley, Donegal fan

I often saw more pushing and shoving coming out of second mass in Crusheen.

Tom McNamara after the infamous
1998 Munster final replay

That's the first time I've seen anybody limping off with a sore finger!

Gene Morgan, Armagh footballer, on an injured teammate

It's like wearing a condom,
you never really get used to it.
Johnny Barr, Dublin footballer,
on the surgical bandage on his left knee

Gaelic football … may seem like a primitive, violent,
mindless exercise in unspeakable brutality. However, to
the initiated enthusiast it is all this and more.
Arthur Mathews, writer and actor

I hear people saying this is 'do-or-die for Kildare', but
I've been hearing that for so long now. Inter-county
football is like a conveyer belt. You step on and you
step off, it still carries on with or without you.
Johnny Doyle, Kildare footballer

Tyrone have a lot of bad players. Brian Dooher is a bad player. I have a very expensive hat and I will eat it on this show if Tyrone win an All-Ireland and Brian Dooher is on the team.

Colm O'Rourke before Tyrone (and Dooher) won the All-Ireland in 2003, in 2005 and again in 2008

And various other unfriendly remarks were made such as 'Me oul' mother would make a better goalie.'

Patrick Kavanagh

The 'Rattler' Byrne: By God, Christy, we'll have to shoot you.

Christy Ring: Oh sure you might as well. Ye've tried everything else.

The standard of name-calling in this club is absolutely diabolical … and we training all winter at it … Make sure the referee can see you, but he can't hear you, right? Then you start, lads. You insult his mother, insult his grandmother, his sisters, his family, every one seeing, breathing generation of them. Insult the shite out of him, annihilate him, lambast him. Make sure that man hits you, you hit the ground.

He gets the line, we get the free.

Jon Kenny as fictitious club manager Timmy Ryan,
in the classic D'unbelievables sketch

When Donal O'Grady smiles
you can hear the cello in *Jaws*.

Keith Duggan, *Irish Times*, on the Limerick hurler

Handbags

It's a reflection, I think, on the wonderful postal service
we have in Northern Ireland and the South.
**Pat Spillane after his postman delivered a letter from Armagh
addressed to 'Pat the Bollocks, Co. Kerry'**

Several of those players out there today aren't even
the cousin of a county footballer
Joe Brolly

Joe Brolly told us the production line was finished in
Kerry. Well, Joe Brolly, what do you think of that?!
Touché. **Kerry's Kieran Donaghy after his team lifted
the Sam Maguire in 2014**

Ollie Murphy is after throwing so many dummies,
you wouldn't see the likes in a crèche.

Kevin Mallon, LMFM, on the Meath footballer

Ref, for Jaysus' sake that's a f**kin penalty. The b******.
He must have no wipers in his glasses.

Eddie Moroney

The first thing I should do is purchase a gun and leave
it to my wife at home. Because if I ever insinuate that
I'm returning to management then I will tell her
to have me shot straight away.

Ger Loughnane

Puke football.

Pat Spillane after Tyrone beat Kerry

in the 2003 All-Ireland semi-final

I think what the Kerry legend really meant to say was
that he had just witnessed 'peak football'. I'm sure it
just came out the wrong way on live TV.

It happens us all, Pat.

Peter Canavan, former Tyrone footballer,

in an *Irish Independent* article

Football was never pukier.

Eamonn Sweeney, *Irish Independent*,
on the 2002 Kerry v Cork Munster semifinal

Maybe we were peaking when we should have been
puking, and puking when we should have
been peaking.

Anthony Daly, former Clare and Dublin hurling manager,
on Dublin's 2014 season

Even in its present form, as a foetus, it probably has a
good chance of making either squad.
**Chris O'Dowd jokes about whether his unborn baby is a
contender for the Roscommon football or camogie teams**

It could be Mayo next year, it could be Kerry…
His principles are completely movable.
Colm O'Rourke on Joe Brolly

Everyone got their money's worth here tonight except
the boys in front of me who got in for nothing
and got paid for it. Good luck!
**Brian Cody, Kilkenny hurling manager, has a dig at the press
after his team beat Galway in the 2006 quarter-final**

The first half was even, the second half was even worse.
Pat Spillane

The next thing I'll be blamed for the Famine!
**Kieran McGeeney, then Kildare football manager,
after a 2011 defeat**

They looked like ducks in thunder.
Joe Brolly on Cavan in their 2007 match against Antrim

There's a lot of politics in hurling.
I don't think Henry Kissinger would have lasted
a week on the Munster Council.
Ger Loughnane

They have a forward line that couldn't
punch holes in a paper bag.
Pat Spillane on the Cavan team

The real problem with the foot and mouth
epidemic, Pat, is that you didn't get it.
Ted Walsh, racehorse trainer, to Pat Spillane

Will somebody please pick up Marty
off the floor there?
**Ger Loughnane after an uncomfortable exchange between
Marty Morrissey and Brian Cody after Kilkenny's win
over Tipperary in the 2009 All-Ireland final**

You both picked Galway.
Sweet mother of all the Brollys.
**Joe Brolly questions the predictions of fellow *Sunday Game*
analysts Pat Spillane and Colm O'Rourke**

Obama's good, but he's not a miracle worker! I'd say he'd sort out Israel, Gaza, Iraq, Iran, Afghanistan and Pakistan long before he'd sort out the Cork hurling panel. All those problems would just be a training ground before you tackle the crisis that is Cork.

Neil Delamere, comedian, in 2009

I swear to God, my mother would be faster than most of those three fellas. And she has a bit of arthritis in the knee.

Pat Spillane

Offaly look like a county who are still living in the dark ages. They're the only team in the modern era where you still see players with fat legs, bellies and arses.

Ger Loughnane

My daughter played football with Rostrevor and she banned me from the sideline because of certain words I was accused of saying, that are clearly misunderstood, and she subsequently apostatised to rowing … she was pretty sure that I could not walk on water.

President Mary McAleese on keeping her enthusiasm for the game in check on the sidelines

This game of Gaelic football has been infiltrated by a load of spoofers and bluffers, people with no experience in some cases of Gaelic football. Fellas with earpieces stuck in their ear, psychologists, statisticians and dieticians.

Pat Spillane

It's pure constipated hurling.

Ger Loughnane

To talk about this not being a game in which to get
revenge, it's absolute poppycock. It's all about revenge.

Liam Hayes, former Meath footballer and journalist,
on the 2013 Donegal v Mayo quarter-final

My father used to have a saying: a big mouth
is good for cooling soup.

Pete Finnerty, former Galway hurler, when Ger Loughnane
questioned Kilkenny's tactics

I would not let anybody into the car park, not to
mention into Croke Park.

Dan Hoare, Munster Council treasurer,
on allowing 'foreign sports' into Croker

If you believe soccer, rugby, Gaelic football,
ladies' football and camogie and other sports
can all be played on the same pitch,
then you have to be a bit of a nitwit.
Taoiseach Bertie Ahern on the need
for a new stadium in Dublin

They're just mushrooms. The more shite you feed them
the faster they'll grow and the better they'll be.
Ger Loughnane about the Clare County board

A former manager commented on some of these
people, referring to mushrooms. But he was being very
unfair to mushrooms: they grow on their own
and they can stand on their own.
Tony Considine, former Clare manager, on his sacking
by the county board

So it was Thailand or Tipperary.
**Anthony Daly, former Clare hurler, on Ger Loughnane's
desire to bring the team somewhere they knew nothing
about hurling; Thailand it was**

He put Conor Mortimer in his pocket and fed him on
farts, as we used to say in primary school.
**Joe Brolly on the Mayo footballer
and his Derry marker Michael McGoldrick**

Football is a game for those not good enough
to play hurling.
Tony Wall, former Tipperary hurler and manager

You know that great piece of Irish literature we were all subjected to when we went to school? *Peig.* Her opening line about herself was that she was an old woman now, with one leg on the bank and the other in the grave – and in a way, it could sum up this Kerry football team.

Pat Spillane on the end of Kerry's 2009 season

If you asked them to shorten a hurley, they'd probably start at the wrong end.

Babs Keating, former Tipperary manager, gives his forthright opinion on a number of journalists

Whenever a team loses there's always a row at half-time, but when they win it's an inspirational speech.

Senator John O'Mahony, former football manager

The International Rules series was a bit like the Vietnam War. Nobody at home cared about it, but everyone involved sure did.

Leigh Matthews, Australian coach

The poet Patrick Kavanagh was also a footballer. Let me rephrase that. He played in goal for Monaghan, which may be a different thing entirely.

Niall Tóibín, comedian and actor

He has an arse like a bag of cement.

Joe Brolly on Derry dual player Geoffrey McGonigle

What's sauce for the Connacht goose should be, but rarely is, sauce for the Kerry gander.

Eamonn Sweeney, *Irish Independent*, on the dismissive attitude to Connacht football

People slag me about my right leg but without it I couldn't use my left.

John Morley, Mayo footballer

You can't win derbies with donkeys.
**Babs Keating on the Cork team before
the 1990 Munster final.**
The donkeys won.

Sheep in a heap.
**Babs Keating's evocative description
of the 1998 Offaly hurlers.**
The sheep went on to win the All-Ireland that year.

Ah sure, he might say we're not a bad oul flock.
**Johnny Pilkington, Offaly hurler, on what Keating might say
to the All-Ireland champions**

Any chance of an autograph?
It's for the wife she really hates you.
Tipp fan to Ger Loughnane

'I'm only doing this to annoy the husband', they say.
Joe Brolly on the Tyrone women who ask him for a selfie

If I went to do that, sure who'd keep manners on
Joe Brolly on *The Sunday Game*? You couldn't expose
the nation to him on his own, could you?
**Colm O'Rourke on whether he had plans
to leave RTE's *The Sunday Game***

Ger Loughnane was fair – he treated us all the same
during training. Like dogs.
Anonymous Clare player

The present Kilkenny team is functional beyond belief.
Ger Loughnane

If Martin [McAleese] was a bit younger he might have lined out himself and I might have one of my embarrassing compulsions to give advice to the referee.

President Mary McAleese at the 2002 Asian GAA Games in Phuket

I was Derry's worst hurler ever. The manager used to shout at me to just kick the feckin' thing!

Joe Brolly

Rule 42

Irishmen have always liked to carry clubs, liked to use them in a fight. Their national game, hurling, gives them a chance to do both … golf is a form of hurling modified by a more cautious race.

From a 1931 *Time* magazine article

Like everyone who has ever seen the game I had a wrong impression of hurling. I thought it was just another excuse for a 'fight'. Many think the same. I have spent hours since Sunday explaining to people in England that there are rules and that the on field discipline is strict and the game is anything but a brawl … as far as television is concerned the danger about hurling is it could be too fast for the camera to follow.

Kenneth Wolstenholme, English sports commentator, 1959

I was in New York last year and I met a fella in a bar – he was on his way home to Kerry from Alaska to see a brother of his who was dying. 'I was listening to one of the games above in Alaska,' he said. 'Twas sub-zero temperatures and I was surrounded by Eskimos. And they hadn't a f**king clue what you were talking about'.

Weeshie Fogarty

Don't think they saw it in Fiji. Still in the dark ages, there, they're still on the wireless. We'll send them a tape but they'll be delighted, like.

Seán Óg Ó hAilpin, Cork hurler,
after his team's 1999 All-Ireland final win

I'm always suspicious of games where you're the only ones that play it.

Jack Charlton, former England soccer international and
Republic of Ireland manager, on hurling

There's one and a half billion people in China that
couldn't give a shite about this game.
**Monaghan football manager Malachy O'Rourke lightens the
mood for Dick Clerkin in the run-up to
an Ulster quarter-final**

Chris, we know you walked in space,
but that's a doddle compared to this game.
**Terence 'Sambo' McNaughton, former Antrim hurler,
to Commander Chris Hadfield, retired Canadian astronaut
and ambassador for Irish tourism**

If you're wondering, she's smiling because she's excited
with Roscommon GAA's prospects this year.
**Chris O'Dowd tweets a picture of himself
with a smiling Beyoncé**

You know these guys flicking golf balls? We had to do that with a ball – that's not round, by the way, it has ridges – on a flat stick, running full pelt, with a guy trying to hit you with a stick.

Golfer Pádraig Harrington gives ex-golfer and US TV host David Feherty some idea of the skills required for hurling

This Fiji performance shows how much fun it would be for us Irish if they put hurling in the Olympics.
I mean, unfair, sure, but fun.

Dara Ó Briain tweets his bright idea after Fiji's victory over Britain in the rugby sevens at the Rio Olympics

[I] wish International Rules was half hurling, half golf.

David O'Doherty, comedian, on Twitter

Before I go any further, I must point out that the game is not a punch up with a ball as an occasional distraction. Gaelic football is about skill and courage. The prime discipline is keeping your eye on the ball, despite the murderous attention of the opposition.

Simon Barnes, *London Times*

'The kids playing Gaelic football have to wear gumshields to protect their teeth. They might get their teeth knocked out otherwise', I say, to the sound of Pablo's jaw hitting the hallow Fechin's turf.
'Also, it's an insurance and health-and-safety thing,'
I add, mumbling only to myself.
How could you translate that in plain English?

Patrick Logue, *Irish Times*, trying to explain Gaelic football to his family's Spanish student before an U11 blitz at St Fechin's of Termonfeckin

If members of Congress aren't behaving,
give 'em a little paddle, a little hurl.
**President Barack Obama tries out his swing
on presentation to him of a specially inscribed hurley**

I know about hurling: I showed up at that school and
they turned to me, every single one and they said 'F**k
off, Yank! You can't play f**kin' hurlin' ...
And they were correct. Never seen a hurl in my life!
They're illegal in thirty-five states of America!
Des Bishop, comedian

It's like gang warfare, innit?
Noel Gallagher, musician, on hurling

This, lads, is a hurley, used in the Irish game of hurling.
A cross between hockey and murder.
**Jason Statham's character kindly gives some chaps a
hands-on crash-course in hurling in the movie *Blitz***

The Irish people are crazy about all kinds of sports,
that's why I'm the greatest also here in Ireland. They
even have their own special games called Irish football
and Irish hurling. They look pretty rough to me, these
football and hurling players. I think I'll stick to boxing.
**Mohammad Ali during his 1972 visit to Ireland
for his Croke Park fight against Al 'Blue' Lewis**

He was using the hurley like a tennis racquet ... he spent ages trying to rise the ball. He came up close to me then and said 'We'll put on a show for these guys'. And then he started, he put the hurl back, and I thought he was going to pole-axe me, you know? He went to hit me and I went to put up my hurl to save myself, and he started fencing with me.

Eddie Keher, former Kilkenny hurling captain, on Mohammad Ali's attempts at hurling, in the IFTA-winning documentary *When Ali Came to Ireland*

We would like to congratulate Limerick on the Championship in Munster hurling ...
We heard all about it.
We don't know what the f**k it is,
but congratulations!
(Bruce then launches into 'Glory Days').

Bruce Springsteen, musician, during his Thomond Park gig in July 2016

This is the game I've been telling you about!
Tom Hanks, actor and film-maker, to his sons as the family
delays their flight to sit in a Shannon Airport bar
and cheer on Galway against Limerick in the
2013 hurling All-Ireland minor semi-final

I went to an Aussie Rules match in Australia and they
were saying that Gaelic football is just like Aussie Rules
but with a different ball. So I've kind of gotten my head
around that. But hurling? Not so much.
Ed Sheeran, musician, prior to his
two 2015 sell-out shows in Croke Park

I am proud to say that I am now a freeman of Dublin.
To look out into this wonderful sea of Irish faces on
this beautiful Irish day I feel like a real 'Dub' today – is
that what I'm supposed to say? Not only that, I know
we have a handy football team.
US President Bill Clinton during his 1995 visit to Dublin

It's all done up now. I'm not even sure there was even
seats. I scored a point but I can't remember
at which end.

**Noel Gallagher on scoring at Croke Park in 1983
for his Manchester club Oisín's, as a teenager**

Joe Rogan: What are they doing?!
This is called hurling, huh?
Dom Irrera: Yeah. The Kilkenny Cats
are the local team.
Joe Rogan: They must hit the f**k out of
each other with those sticks.

**Joe Rogan, UFC commentator, and comedian Dom Irrera
watch hurling for the first time**

You know if it's an Irish sport you know two things
– you know it's f**king crazy and you know there's
nobody stretching.
Bill Burr, US comedian, discovers the ancient
Irish sport of hurling

Hurling looks a bit like a cross between
lacrosse and second degree murder.
David Feherty

She saw it on television on Sky, she said 'I'm not quite
sure how I got it', but she said it was wonderful. She
made a side-to-side motion with her head saying it was
very fast and it was a wonderful game … I'm not sure
whether it was Offaly v Kilkenny or Wexford v Dublin,
we didn't go into detail on that … but the fact of the
matter is that she says she saw it … and she said
it was a wonderful game.
Liam O'Neill, former GAA President,
on dinner conversation with the Queen

He said hurling was a bit like the Scottish game, shinty, and I told him it was, but that there were a few differences. I told him how we lift the ball and catch it in the air and try to strike it faster but he was surprised that there were not a lot more injuries.

Anthony Cunningham, Galway hurling manager, on his chat with Prince Charles

It doesn't get more republican than Setanta. Jesus, the first time I heard that word cried out over the loud speaker I thought I was going to see a man fly into Croke Park on a white-winged horse, like the Pegasus!

Des Bishop on Cork hurler Setanta Ó hAilpín

The rough equivalent of 30 million Americans watching a regional lacrosse game.

Forbes **magazine on the**

2007 Munster hurling final in Thurles

Saw some hurling on TV last night so I'd just like to
say congratulations, Ireland, on any of you
being left alive.

A tweet from Chris Addison, comedian and actor

English guy in pub who's watched the hurling on Sky
Sports; 'Mad sport, it's a bit *Game of Thrones*, innit?'

Joe O'Shea, writer and broadcaster, on Twitter

Just watched 5 mins of hurling, WTF is going on?
There's a goalkeeper, but they keep smashing it
over the bar. How the f**k does he save that?

**Mike Kay tweets while watching
Sky's hurling coverage**

Why's a hockey goalkeeper kitted up like Darth Vader
whilst a hurling goalkeeper just stands there
in his shorts and t-shirt?

Paul Jones joins the Twitter storm

All-England champions Dublin.
Sky Sports anchor, Mike Wedderburn,
makes a bit of a slip-up

Still hiding under a rock after my horrendous gaffe
about the All-Ireland GAA final. Apologies to all –
please let me visit still.
Clare Tomlinson, Sky Sports presenter, after she referred to
the 'All-England' Dublin v Mayo 2016 football final

Marketing the sports to a broader constituency is
a problem, especially in the US, where 'hurling' is
something you do when you have a
violent stomach upset.
Frank McNally, journalist, in his book
Xenophobe's Guide to the Irish

I was at a dinner party only the other week with the Queen and … [she] was particularly strong on 'Look after your points, look after your points'.

Dara Ó Briain jokes about the fervour in London in the run-up to their 2013 championship match against Mayo

I'll tell you what I like about Ireland, as well, is that you're clever … in that you've made sports that nobody else wants to play … You're never going to have a World Cup in hurling, are you? … Al Qaeda wouldn't even do f**king hurling!

John Bishop, comedian

Susie Dent: A 'slee-oh-tar' is a hard, leather-covered ball used in the game of hurling.

Nick Hewer: I think it's actually pronounced 'slither'.

It's a scoreless draw for the *Countdown* presenters in the hurling pronunciation game

These hurling fellas don't even wear gloves.
Fingers like steel.
Joey Barton, soccer player, tweets his admiration

In what sport do you get eighty-thousand people
cheering on plumbers, carpenters and teachers in a
national final? Gaelic football, of course!
BBC Breakfast **as presenter Mike Bushell, investigates the
growing popularity of Gaelic football in the UK**

For Gaels, what the rest of the world understands as
'sport' is not sport at all. The world doesn't know
what it's missing.
Joe Brolly

Up for the
Match

The wind is strong. It's with Kerry as a straw hat rolls like a wheel across the field out towards the Nally Stand. 'Twould make a great souvenir for someone. It's now slowing to a halt, it's coming to a rest thirty-seven yards from where the Cusack Stand used to be. Daire Ó Cinnéide, no interest in hats now, ready to take the free ... the free is already taken to Liam Hassett – over the straw hat, over the 21 and he's sent it wide.

Micheál Ó Muircheartaigh

I don't want to be biased,
but what was the referee at there?
Sean Walsh, Galway Bay FM

And Dickie Watch looks at his Murphy.
Liam Spratt

The cigarettes are being lit here in the commentary box.
The lads are getting anxious, it's a line ball down there
to Clare and who's to take it? ... Will ye put 'em out
lads ye'll feckin' choke me!
Matthew McMahon, Clare FM commentator,
at the 1995 hurling All-Ireland

It's all over ... Clare are ... Jeeeesus!!
Matthew McMahon overcomes the fumes

Is the ref going to finally blow his whistle? ...
No, he's going to blow his shaggin' nose!
Radio Kilkenny commentator on Kilkenny v Wexford
National League match

… and Brian Dooher is down injured. And while he is down I'll tell you a little story. I was in Times Square in New York last week, and I was missing the Championship back home. So I approached a newsstand and I said 'I suppose ye wouldn't have *The Kerryman*, would you?' To which the Egyptian behind the counter turned to me, he said 'Do you want the North Kerry edition or the South Kerry edition?' He had both, so I bought both. Dooher is back on his feet.

Micheál Ó Muircheartaigh entertains listeners while Tyrone's Brian Dooher receives treatment

Jaysus, they're lovely sandwiches. Billy, will ya go down there and find out who made those sandwiches?

Liam Spratt to Billy Byrne, South East Radio

The only time I ever made the front page of the *Irish Times* it was because I had lost my skirt.

**Angela Downey, Kilkenny camogie player,
on how a wardrobe malfunction got better press
than her legendary playing career**

When you play in a packed Croke Park, you can hear nothing, not even your teammates calling for the ball … some things become peripheral. To be honest, I didn't even notice that it was raining until it was mentioned after the game.

Gregory McCartan, Down footballer

Is it raining? I hadn't noticed

Well, there is a streaker on the field now. He must be a Kilkenny man because he is quite happy with the situation right now ... If the streaker doesn't mind, the ball will be going over in his direction now. He sees the danger, he's moving out the field towards open territory … The stewards are moving in on him now from all sides. The hurlers are ignoring it. He's now gone past the centre of the field … Níl fhios agam cad as a tháinig sé. B'fhéidir piobaire sídh slí Gleann Molúra é … He's dodging his way, trying to get away now from the maor. He's made a good run. He's on the fifty yard line on the other side of the field. He's brought to the ground. Play has been halted here. This is not the referee's business. He is quite happy to wait until the pitch is clear. Tá an streaker ag imeacht.

Micheál Ó Muircheartaigh on the 2003 Kilkenny v Wexford hurling final, just after a Henry Shefflin goal

Was the traffic bad on your way up, Billy?
About the same, Liam. I was in your car.
Liam Spratt and Billy Byrne, South East Radio

And it's in the back of the net,
but there's a free out to be taken by I dunno …
Brian Connolly … Kenneally … Connolly …
Will ya kick the ball! … Me false teeth are coming out.
I can't keep them in!
Eddie Moroney

People have said to me already you did
Bill Clinton and Monica Lewinsky a favour:
you took them off the front page.
**Ref Jimmy Cooney on ending the 1998 hurling semi-final
replay four minutes early**

Now, I wouldn't overdo whatever you put on it.
I wouldn't have it coming out to the edges. Just within.
Sort of like a football pitch, the lines are there. Outside
it, nothing else. On the pitch, the essential … Cúpla
tomato now … they wouldn't be evenly cut but they'd
be cut so that they'd rest on it. Cúpla ceann. I would
place those like the team would line out, not too near
each other … Now it's made now, except to divide it
into two equal halves. I don't like the modern idea of
making two triangles out of it. Bread was never meant
to be triangular, 'twas meant to be square like
a good field, a square field.

**Micheál Ó Muircheartaigh's commentary on how to make the
perfect 'hang sangwich', from the *Irish Times* video**

I know one swallow doesn't make a summer, but if you
see one swallow at least you know the
summer's coming.

Cyril Farrell, former Galway hurling manager

We were staying in the Horse & Jockey. Myself and Ciaran Whelan were kicking a ball around the car park …Colm Meaney shows up. At that time *The Snapper* was huge – it was everywhere – but he was also in *Star Trek* …Vinnie [Murphy] is shifting about in the [hotel room] window with a bathrobe on him. Window opens, Vinnie drops the bathrobe and goes 'Here, Colm, can you beam that up?!' And Colm Meaney, fair play to him, goes, 'Vinnie, you concentrate on the match!'

Senan Connell, Dublin footballer, on the run-up to the 2001 Dublin v Kerry match

Back when I played football I was a very serious man, and I asked my coach at the time, Kevin McStay, what he thought of me as a footballer. And he said, 'You're a f**king joke!' And that was really what brought comedy into my life.

Chris O'Dowd

Mary Robinson was President at the time, and we were told have your socks up when she shakes your hand or it's £50 per player of a fine!

**Daithi Regan, Offaly hurler,
on the 1995 All-Ireland hurling final**

There are people drinking and barbeques and music blaring. At one stage you couldn't nearly see the far goals with the smoke coming from the barbeques.

**Emlyn Mulligan, Leitrim football captain, on his team's
victorious trip to the Bronx during the 2013 championship**

If he hits the ball like he did in the first half, this will end up in Clonliffe College. Yes, it's gone over Hill 16 and out over the railway. That slíotar will play no more hurling today.

Micheál Ó Muircheartaigh

That would have been great.
Of all of them that's the one I wanted to be true.
I double-checked the numbers.
**Lar Corbett, Tipperary hurler,
on the bizarre rumour that he'd won the lotto**

In those days, there was one microphone which covered
the commentator, the crowd, the band, everything.
This was a round thing that was up over my head in the
box. Lightning was flashing off this and going along the
wires. It could have been frightening but the match was
so good you didn't notice it.
**Michael O'Hehir on 1939's 'Thunder and Lightning'
hurling final**

The stopwatch has stopped. It's up to God and the
referee now. The referee is Pat Horan. God is God.
Micheál Ó Muircheartaigh

I can see by the look on his face that he's not too happy
... even though he has his back to me!

Liam Spratt

This is full duck or no dinner now... The ball is sailing
down towards Drumcondra Road. Any sign of Bertie
Ahern in Fagan's I wonder ... A goal! What did I tell
you? Micheál Kelly has won the Nicky Rackard Cup
for Roscommon in the most incredible
situation of all times!

Willie Hegarty

I see John O'Donnell dispensing water on the sideline.
Tipperary sponsored by a water company, Cork
sponsored by a tea company. I wonder will they meet
later for afternoon tea.

Micheál Ó Muircheartaigh

If any team other than Dublin, Kerry, Mayo or Tyrone wins the Sam Maguire Cup in 2017, I will ride a horse naked through the victorious county. Needless to say I don't expect to have to fulfil that promise.

Pat Spillane

The great thing about the GAA is that you can't change your allegiance so wherever you're born is the team you'll support all your life. The thing about being from a county that doesn't win the All-Ireland all that often is that when you do win it gives you a licence to go wild and stage some kind of Roman orgy!

Neil Delamere

We're champions of f**king Ireland!
John 'Bubbles' O'Dwyer, Tipperary hurler, gets a little over-excited and drops the f-bomb on live tv

I remember saying to people, 'Jeez, will ye let me through or they'll give the cup to someone else.'
Clare captain, Anthony Daly, on his struggle to lift the Liam MacCarthy cup in 1995

Over the bar was the place for it, lads! Over the bar was the place for it! ... Timmy Moloney who's going to be getting married later on in the month. 'Twill be another heavy day, I'd say ... There's men being kicked and booted all over it! ... Where did that go, lads? Wide? ... The referee is looking around and acting the mickey! ... What a victory! Oh, Mother of God, there'll be a big night in the Glen!
Eddie Moroney

You're very welcome to Limerick during the week.

House party: Monday night, Tuesday night.

Limerick hurler Stephen Lucey makes
President Mary McAleese an offer she can't refuse
before the 2007 All-Ireland final against Kilkenny.
(Limerick lost, putting the kibosh on party plans.)

I actually didn't make it to Coppers that night,
but that's well documented.

Bryan Cullen, Dublin football captain, about his famous
'See you all in Coppers' line when lifting the
Sam Maguire in 2011

It was more of a committee. There are about three or four lads together and they go to the local [shop] like Sean Hussey's in Tralee. And a county board official comes along. And a Kerry Group official comes along. The three players will pick out this suit and the county board official and Kerry Group official will pick out this suit. Sean Hussey will say no, 'No, no. I think the boys' suit. We'll go with that. And we all go away thinking it is our suit and we show up at the hotel, on the day, and it is the other suit. Really it's nothing to do with the players, in truth.

Paul Galvin on picking out suits for All-Ireland Final Day

There won't be a cow milked in Clare tonight!
**Marty Morrissey on Clare's 1992 Munster football final
win over Kerry**

There won't be a cow milked in Finglas tonight!
**Keith Barr, Dublin footballer,
after a club semi-final win by Erin's Isle**

I'm not a guy that is going to lose the run of himself.
I'm nearly sixteen stone so I am not going to go
floating anywhere.

**John Evans, Tipperary football manager,
on their first league title in thirty-eight years**

They lost nothing today, except pride and, of course,
the Connacht title.

Marty Morrissey on Mayo's 2003 defeat against Galway

One parish sometimes challenges another; they pick
out ten, twelve or twenty players of a side, and the prize
is generally a barrel or two of ale, which is brought into
the field and drunk off by the victors on the spot.

John Dunton, 1698

He [Mossy Keane, Roy's father] came to me later in the night, and he was holding a pint glass, half full, and he come over to me and he said 'I heard you never drank. Could that be true?' and from the tone of his voice he wasn't inclined to believe that that could be true. So I said 'It never appealed to me. It doesn't even look attractive' ... In fairness to him, he considered what I said, he lifted up his glass and 'twas half full, and he looked at it from the right and from the left, and looked at it from underneath, and then he came back to me and he said, 'Would you believe, Micheál, I have an entirely different opinion.'

Micheál Ó Muircheartaigh, the famous teetotaller

We'll circle the wagons and drive on, and that starts
in the Horse & Jockey.

Babs Keating on how his Tipp team would cope with losing

One day we were beaten and I said to him,
'Well, Doc [McGrath], what do you reckon now?'
'I'll tell you one thing now, Jackie,' he said, 'nice guys
marry nice girls but they don't win Munster finals.
And to be fair to ye, ye all married lovely girls.'

**Jackie O'Gorman, former Clare hurler,
on commiserations from the team doctor**